This is Me!

By Sonia Sharpe

Library For All Ltd.

This is Me!

First published 2023

Published by Library For All Ltd
Email: info@libraryforall.org
URL: libraryforall.org

Our Yarning logo design by Jason Lee, Bidjipidji Art

Original illustrations by Jasurbek Ruzmat

This is Me!
Sharpe, Sonia
ISBN: 978-1-923110-13-7
SKU03373

This is Me!

We respect and honour Aboriginal
and Torres Strait Islander Elders past,
present and future. We acknowledge
the stories, traditions and living cultures
of Aboriginal and Torres Strait Islander
peoples on this land and commit to
building a brighter future together.

G'day, my name is Cooper and I want to tell you about me!

I'm from the Awabakal Nation of Newcastle, New South Wales.

I like to learn from our Elders because their lives were so different to ours now.

This is me!

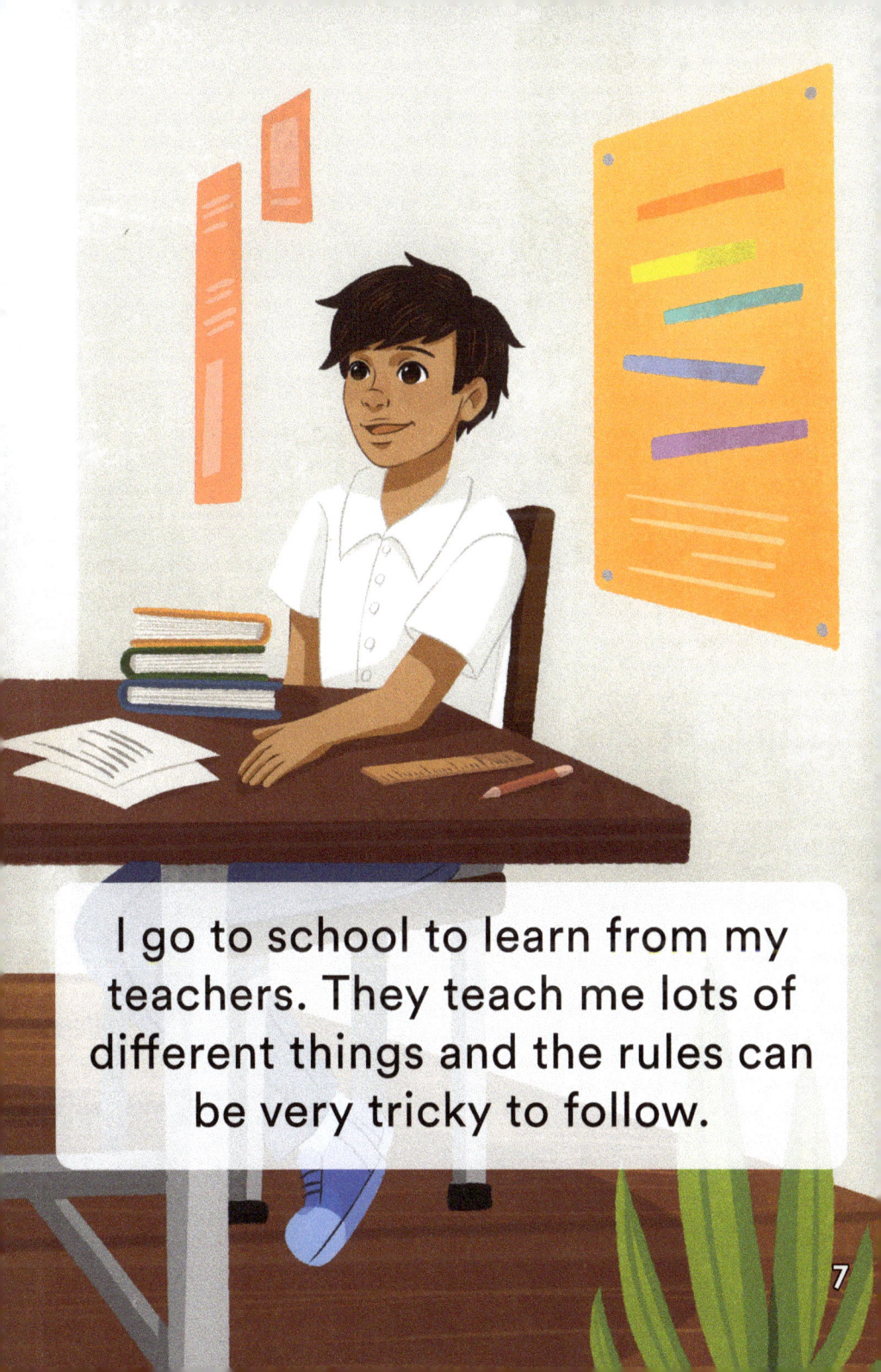

I go to school to learn from my teachers. They teach me lots of different things and the rules can be very tricky to follow.

This is me!

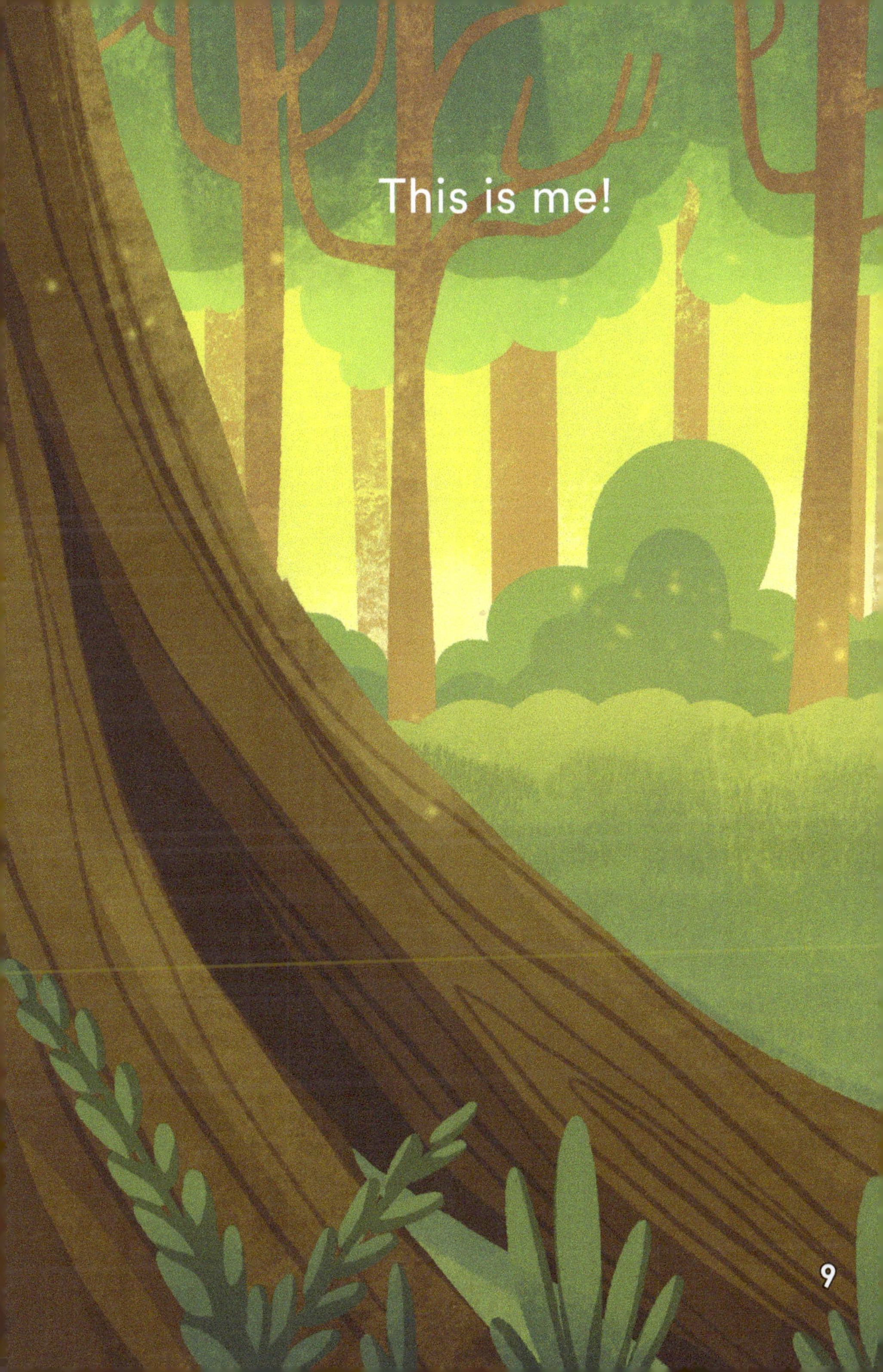

After school, I like to
ride my motorbike
and play footy with
my friends.

This is me!

At home, I live with my family.

I have lots of brothers and sisters and we like to go hunting together, because we love to eat kangaroo.

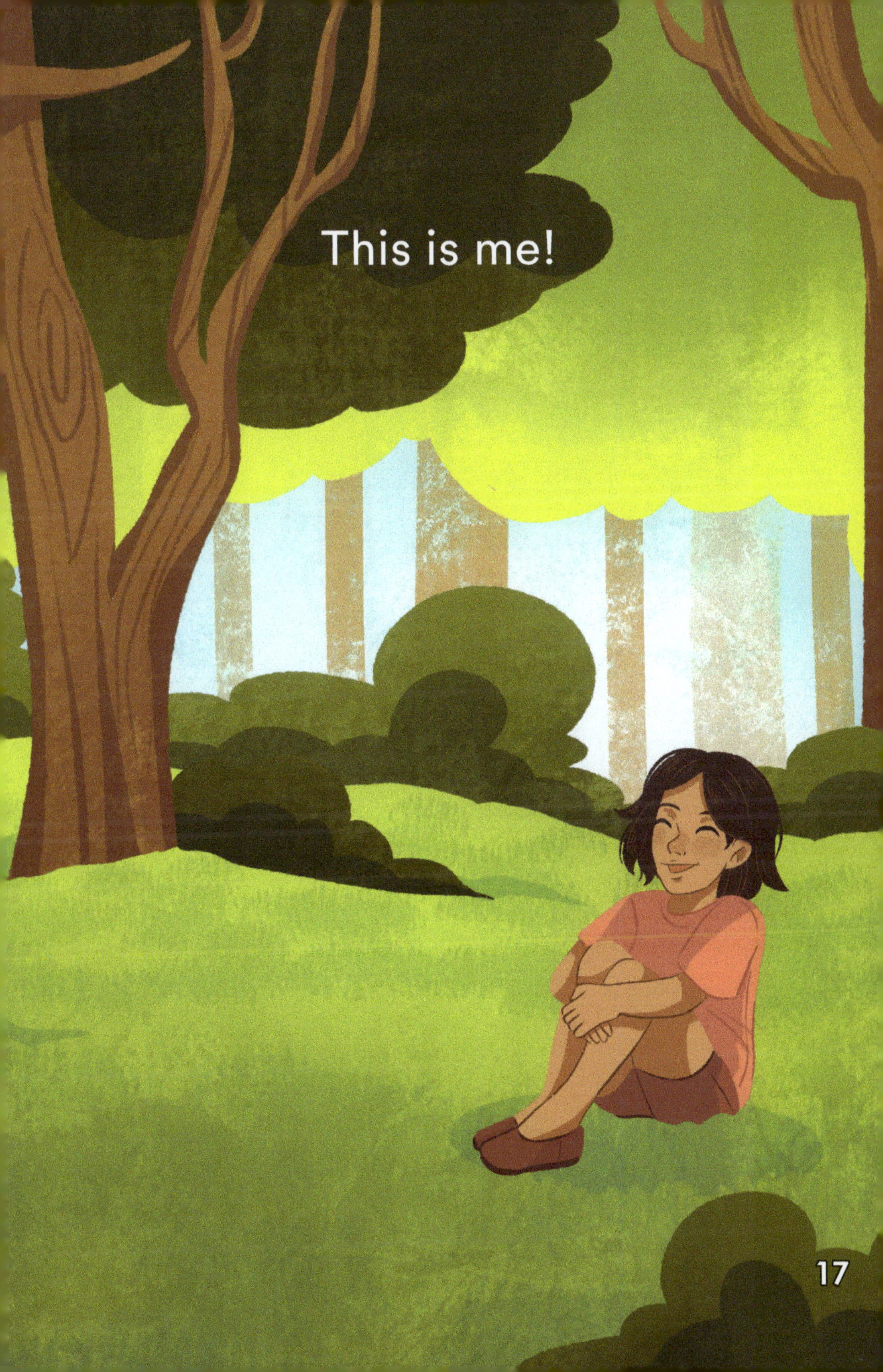

This is me!

Mum and Dad use all parts of
the kangaroo, so nothing goes to
waste, just like our old people did.

This is us!

You can use these questions to talk about this book with your family, friends and teachers.

What did you learn from this book?

Describe this book in one word.
Funny? Scary? Colourful? Interesting?

How did this book make you feel when you finished reading it?

What was your favourite part of this book?

download our reader app
getlibraryforall.org

About the author

Sonia was born in Newcastle on Awabakal Land and loves spending time with her family. She adores being around her precious grandchildren — seeing their perspective on the world they live in keeps her young. As a child she loved *Tin Tin* and *Asterix*.

Darwin

NORTHERN TERRITORY

QUEENSLAND

WESTERN AUSTRALIA

SOUTH AUSTRALIA

NEW SOUTH WALES

Brisbane

Perth

Adelaide

Sydney

ACT
Canberra

Author's Country

VICTORIA
Melbourne

TASMANIA
Hobart

Our Yarning

Want to discover more books from this collection? Our Yarning is a collection of books written by Aboriginal and Torres Strait Islander peoples across Australia.

We know that children learn better, and enjoy reading more, when they see themselves in the stories, characters and illustrations of the books they read.

To download the app, visit the Google Play Store on any Android device and search 'Our Yarning'.

libraryforall.org

www.ingramcontent.com/pod-product-compliance
Lightning Source LLC
Chambersburg PA
CBHW042345040426
42448CB00019B/3409